Contents

Some words are shown in bold, **like this**. They are explained in the glossary on page 23.

What are senses?

Humans can see, hear, smell, touch, and taste.

These are your **senses**.

Super Senses

Special Animal Senses

Mary Mackill

www.raintreepublishers.co.uk
Visit our website to find out more information about **Raintree** books.

To order:
☎ Phone 44 (0) 1865 888112
🖹 Send a fax to 44 (0) 1865 314091
💻 Visit the Raintree Bookshop at **www.raintreepublishers.co.uk** to browse our catalogue and order online.

First published in Great Britain by Raintree, Halley Court, Jordan Hill, Oxford OX2 8EJ, part of Harcourt Education.
Raintree is a registered trademark of Harcourt Education Ltd.

Editorial: Kate Bellamy
Design: Jo Hinton-Malivoire and bigtop
Picture Research: Hannah Taylor and Fiona Orbell
Production: Helen McCreath

Originated by Chroma Graphics (Overseas) Pte. Ltd
Printed and bound in China by
South China Printing Company

ISBN 1 406 20025 5 (hardback)
ISBN 978 1 406 20025 6 (hardback)
10 09 08 07 06
10 9 8 7 6 5 4 3 2 1
ISBN 1 406 20032 8 (paperback)
ISBN 978 1 406 20032 4 (paperback)
11 10 09 08 07
10 9 8 7 6 5 4 3 2 1

British Library Cataloguing in Publication Data
Mackill, Mary
Special Animal Senses – (Super Senses)
573.8'7
A full catalogue record for this book is available from the British Library.

Acknowledgements
The publishers would like to thank the following for permission to reproduce photographs:
Alamy Images pp. **5** (eWILDz), **9** (Imagestate), **13** (Kevin Schafer), **17**, **23a** (Robert Harding Picture Library); Corbis pp. **7**, **10**, **22tl**, **24l** (royalty free), **12**, **22tr**, **24r** (Gallo Images; Nigel J. Dennis), **4**, **23c** (Norbert Schafer), **6** (Tom Stewart); Getty Images pp. **20** (Digital Vision), **14** (Photodisc), **11**, **15**, **22bl**, **24cl** (The Image Bank); naturepl.com pp. **18**, **23b** (John Downer), **21** (Michael Pitts), **8** (Peter Reese); Photolibrary.com pp. **16**, **23d**; Science Photo Library pp. **19**, **22br**, **24cr** (Georgette Douwma).

Cover photograph reproduced with permission of Alamy Images/Martin Harvey.

Every effort has been made to contact copyright holders of any material reproduced in this book. Any omissions will be rectified in subsequent printings if notice is given to the publishers.

The paper used to print this book comes from sustainable resources.

Disclaimer
All the Internet addresses (URLs) given in this book were valid at the time of going to press. However, due to the dynamic nature of the Internet, some addresses may have changed, or sites may have changed or ceased to exist since publication. While the author and publishers regret any inconvenience this may cause readers, no responsibility for any such changes can be accepted by either the author or the publishers.

Did you know most animals have the same senses as you?

Why are senses important?

Your **senses** tell you about the world around you.

Animals live in many different places.

Their senses tell them what is
around them, too.

Super spotters

Some animals have a super **sense** of sight!

Owls are good at seeing in the dark.

A chameleon can look in two
different ways at the same time!

Super Listeners

Some animals are good at hearing.

Elephants can hear sounds that are too low for us to hear.

Some animals, like foxes, have large ears that they can move.

They listen for sounds all around them.

Super sniffers

Animals that can not see well often have a good **sense** of smell.

An aardvark uses its special nose to smell for food.

Ants follow a smell to find their way home.

Super tasters

Some animals have a super **sense** of taste.

An earthworm has taste buds all over its body!

Did you know a butterfly can taste with its feet?

Super feelers

whisker

Animals use touch to tell them where they are.

A catfish has lots of **whiskers** to touch things around it.

antennae

A snail uses its **antennae** to touch.

If it does not know what something is, it will go back into its shell.

Super travellers

Pigeons have a **sense** called **homing**.

A special part of their brain tells them which way to fly home.

A turtle can swim a long way home using its homing sense.

Super bodies

Some animals have bodies that **sense** light.

A starfish moves around by following light.

This fish's body can sense colour as well as light.

It can change its colour to match what is around it!

Super sense detective!

Which super **sense** belongs to which animal?

tasting

homing

hearing

smelling

Find the answers on page 24.

Glossary

 **antennae** (say *an-tan-ay*)   pair of feelers that some animals have on their heads

 **homing**   special sense that some animals have to find their way home

 **sense**   something that helps you to see, touch, taste, smell, and hear the things around you

 **whiskers**   long hairs that grow around the mouths of some animals

Index

Answers to super sense detective:

hearing   tasting   homing   smelling

Note to Parents and Teachers

Reading for information is an important part of a child's literacy development. Learning begins with a question about something. Help children think of themselves as investigators and researchers by encouraging their questions about the world around them. Read the chapter headings. Look at the pictures. Talk about what you think the information on the pages will be about. Then read the text to find out if your predictions were correct. Think of some questions you could ask about the topic, and discuss where you might find the answers. Assist children in using the picture glossary and the index to practice new vocabulary and research skills.